MAGIC MOVING IMAGES

animated optical illusions

Colin Ord

CE

Published by tarquin publications
Suite 74, 17 Hollywell Hill
St Albans
England
AL1 4DT
www.tarquinbooks.com

Copyright © Colin Ord, 2006

ISBN: 1899618740

Printed in the United Kingdom

Introduction

Moving images first appeared in the 19th century as simple optical devices such as the Thaumatrope and the Zoetrope.

The process of displaying sequences of still images in rapid succession – to show apparent motion – is the basis of early film animation and motion pictures.

Creating a Magic Moving Image

To create each magic moving image, an animation consisting of six frames is first produced. Then, each of the six frames is sliced into a pattern of alternating black lines and spaces. A special grating determines the width of the lines and spaces.

The six sliced images are offset from each other by one line width, and they are finally combined to create one complex image that appears on the page.

The special grating initially used to slice the frames is reproduced on an acetate overlay. When the overlay is placed on the page, a solid image becomes visible. With a continuous sideways movement of the overlay, all six frames of the animation are shown in quick succession and the image appears to move.

Preparing the Acetate Overlay

To see the magic moving images you will need a special acetate overlay. (One is provided at the start of the book)

This overlay can be easily removed by cutting along the dotted line marked with a ✂ image.

Viewing the Animations

Place the overlay onto the magic moving image with its lines running vertically.

Very slowly move the overlay sideways across the page, keeping it flat and parallel with the image.

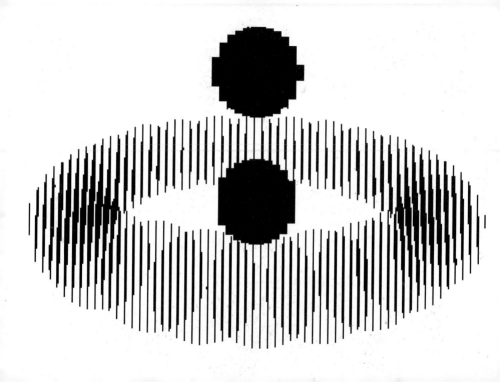

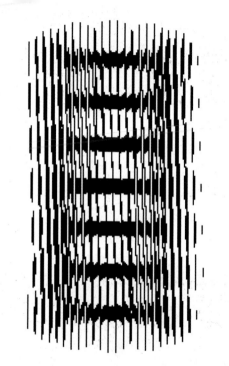

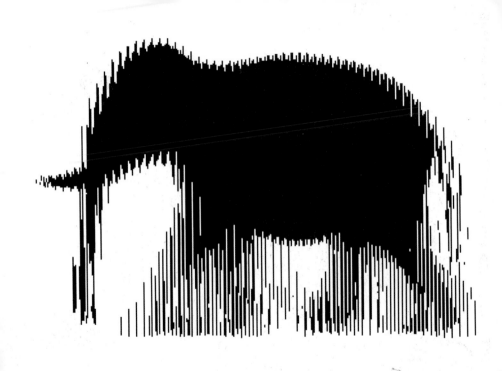

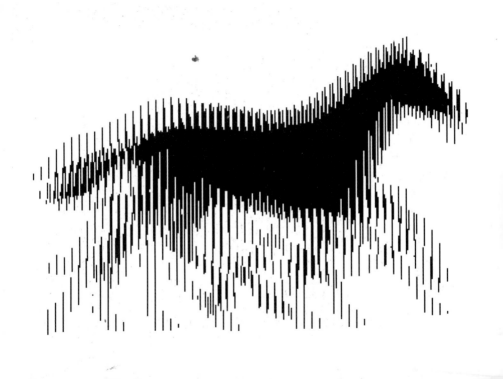

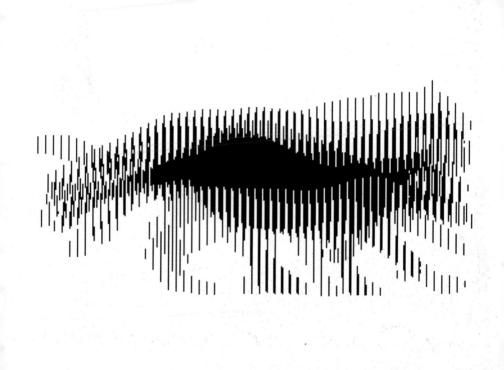

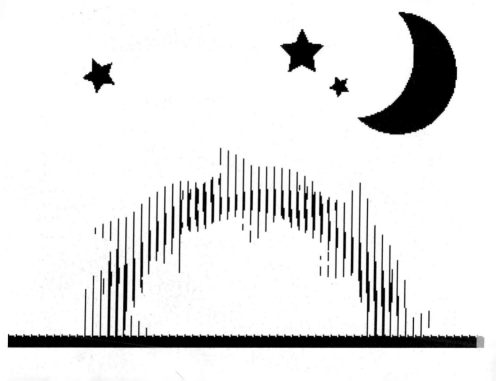

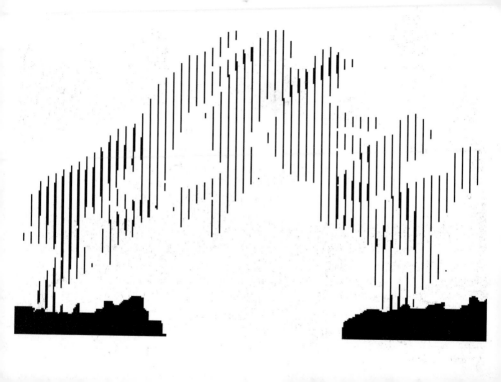

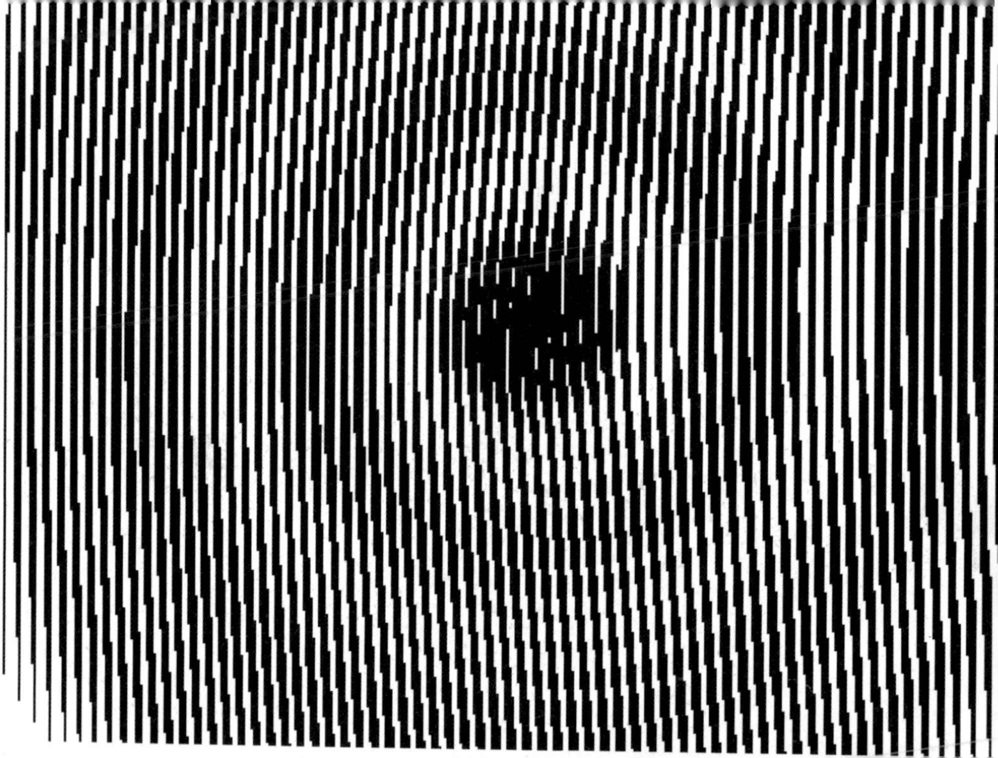

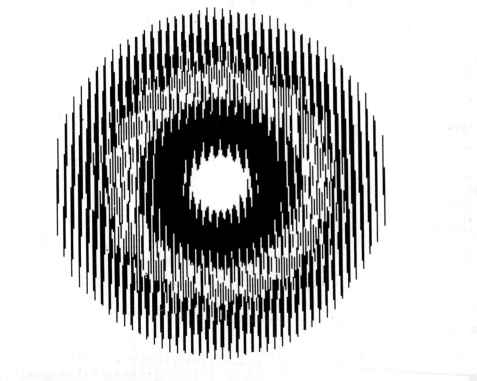

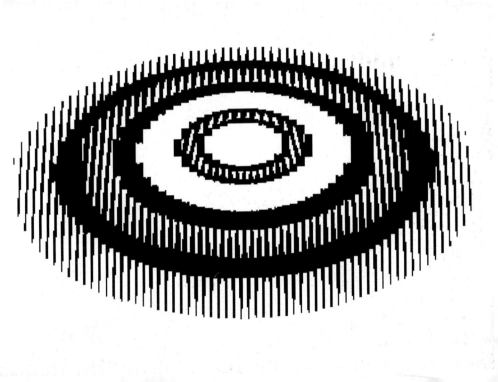

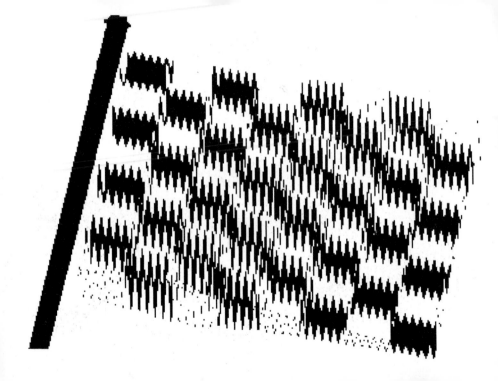

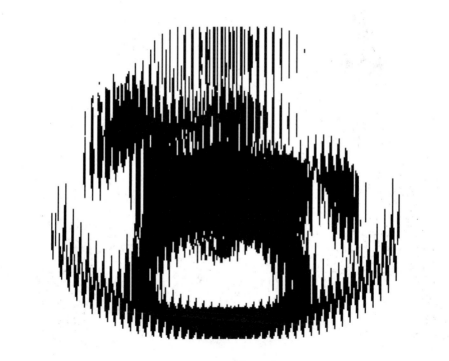

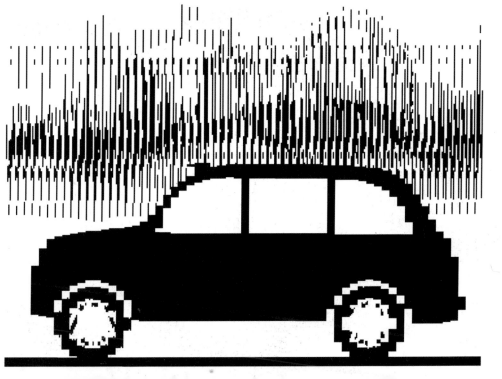

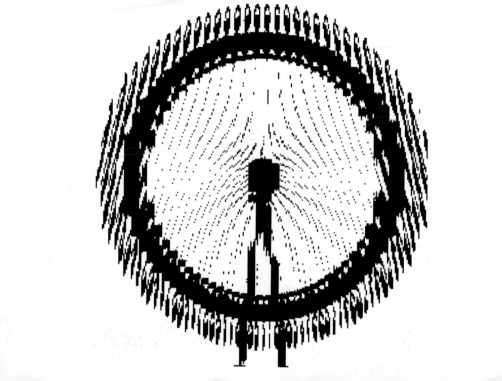

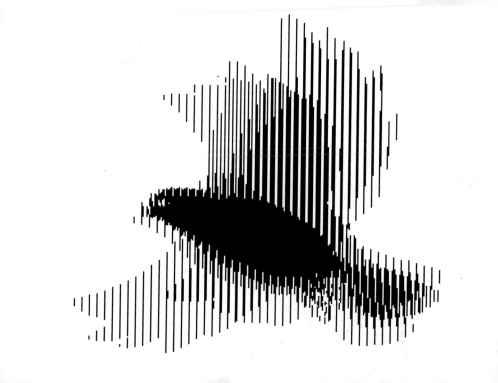

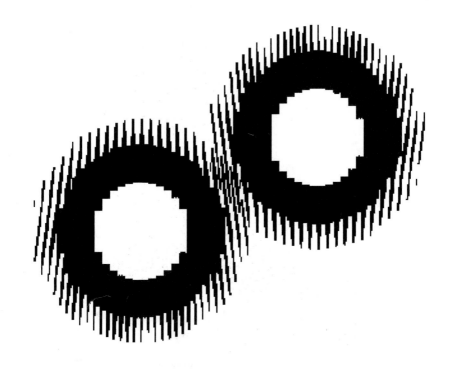

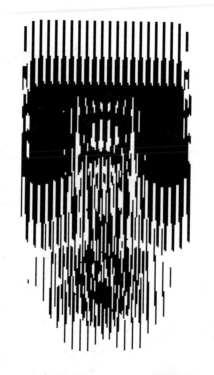

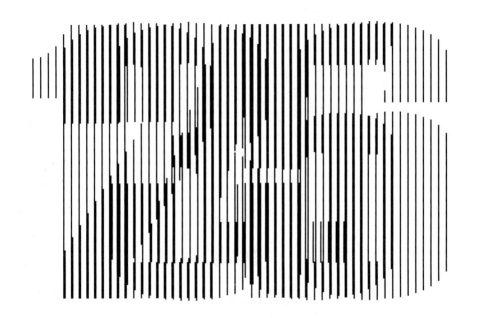

3D
3D Balls
3D Cross
3D Helix
3D Cube

Animals
Elephant Striding
Horse Galloping
Cat Pouncing
Dolphin Jumping

Human
Walking The Dog
Man Cycling
Man Jumping
Man Rowing

Geometric
Crazy Spiral
Trefoil Rotate
Geometric Spin 1
Geometric Spin 2

Generic interest
Flag Waving
Rocking Horse
Clock Time
London Taxi Ride
London Landmark
Windmill Turning
Bird Flapping
Gears Turning
Piston Working
Countdown